MW00935682

Your Jar of Wisdom

Your Jar of Wisdom

Kailee Billerbeck

Alexis,

Remember to always follow your dreams and live in suit of your passions. someone has to do it... why not you?

Love, Kailee

Kailee B

For all of the girls who are learning to overcome life's adversities and want to learn how to look at the world through optimistic eyes.

Acknowledgements

This book would not have been possible without all of the assistance and support I have received from some extraordinary people.

First, this simple message does not express the extent of my debt to my amazing editor, Candace Wilson, who spent hours reviewing my work and talking me through the publishing process.

Second, thank you to my parents, Jason and Renee. I have received an interminable amount of wisdom, love and support from you guys that made writing this book a tangible aspiration.

Third, thank you to Tellis Aucoin for creating the image on the cover and for her optimistic, creative spirit that has inspired me to be who I am and to follow my dreams. You have taught me how to appreciate life even in its darkest forms.

Fourth, thank you to all of the girls who gave me lessons they wanted to see in the book: Libby, Kendall, Savannah, Payton, Malena, Isabelle, and Sydnee. And to all the girls who have come to my business, l.a.f.s. (learning about friends, family, future, and school), and allowed me to share my wisdom. You each inspired me to write this book and have been my driving force.

Most importantly thank you to my sister, Mariah, for being my biggest cheerleader. I am who I am because of your friendship and how you look up to me. Thank you for making l.a.f.s. a success and being such a bright light in my life. I have no doubt that you will do amazing things.

And thank you to the amazing people around me who have all lent a helping hand in making me who I am today and given me the strength to be who I am.

Table of Contents

Introduction

Your jar of wisdom is something that lies inside of you. We all have one. This jar is full of lessons we learn as the years go on, as we fight battles, and as we grow into ourselves.

This is not your typical book. With many books, you have to find a large sum of time to sit and read it, but not with this one.

This book stemmed from the business I founded, l.a.f.s. (learning about friends, family, future, and school). In this business I plan activities for the girls that apply to the lesson I am going to teach them. We have one of these sessions once a week. I have been able to share some lessons I have learned through my lifetime and meet with the girls in groups and one on one to help them through some of life's many struggles.

Since I cannot meet with every one of you when you are experiencing hardships or need some wisdom, I have bound all my wisdom in this book. Every chapter is tailored to help you with different parts of life you may encounter. And when you come across these things and are in need of some advice, you can look in the table of contents and find the lesson that best corresponds to your situation.

The first part of the book begins with "You feel". There are different emotions you will feel and I walk you through them. The second portion of the book begins with "How to". These are instructional lessons that help you improve your character and learn how to deal with life in its many forms. You can sit and read it all at once, but I recommend reading the lessons as they appear in your life.

You Feel

You feel afraid to do something

Maybe you are running for a position in a club, writing a book, starting a business, doing a speech, giving a presentation, or following your dreams. Life can be extremely scary sometimes.

It is hard to put yourself out there. It is scary to do something you are not used to. But I dare you to take the leap. You have a comfort zone, made of things you are comfortable doing and a growth zone where you put yourself out there and try something a little uncomfortable. In order to grow, you must take that leap towards your growth zone.

Being scared is normal. We all feel scared. What sets successful people apart from the rest is having the courage to take that leap. You can be successful. You have all the potential. Sometimes we may initially fail, but that is okay. I have failed and you will fail- the best of us do. But keep trying. Learn from your failures because soon you will win. Don't let failure dampen your spirits; instead, let failure lift them up. You *will* find your time to win.

The leap is difficult. There is no easy way to do it.

But in life, if you put your mind to something, there is nothing you cannot do. If you do the things that scare you, they eventually become part of the comfort zone. This allows us to do, experience, learn, and live. Each of these special aspects can be added to your jar of wisdom.

You feel confused about who your real friends are

Sometimes it is so hard to see who our real friends are. You feel like nobody understands who you really are and have no idea who to trust or turn to. Even when you are surrounded by many people, you can still feel alone and confused as to who really cares.

Looking for true friends is simple. Surround yourself with people who make you feel good.

Nobody should ever make you feel like you don't belong or like you have to work for their friendship. Friendship is a special thing that we tend to take for granted and misconstrue. Friends are there to enjoy the good times and walk beside us during the bad times. Yet, sometimes we begin looking for friends for the wrong reasons.

It doesn't matter what others think. Be around people who you truly know have your back and who understand you. Most of the time, we know who our true friends are, we are just blinded by misconception. We begin to think we should find friends that make us more popular. Let me be the first to inform, popularity is not a title to strive for. Strive for happiness. Be with people who build you up, not break you down.

You are the only one that knows how people make you feel. You hold the key to your own world of bliss. Don't settle for people who make you hurt, search for those who bring out the best in you.

You feel frustrated with someone

We tend to become upset with people when we feel like our voices are not being heard. We begin to raise our voices. Words are spat into the air that cannot be taken back. Our blood boils and our stomachs twist into pretzel-like knots. We become confused about how someone cannot see where we are coming from.

Inhale. Exhale.

Frustration is controllable. Frustration is miscommunication. Take the time to really put yourself in someone else's shoes. Try your best to understand where they are coming from.

Being calm is key to communicating in a sensitive situation. It's important to control your emotion and sympathize with the other person. Taking accountability where it is due is extremely important and make sure to explain where you are coming from.

We tend to get so caught up in proving our points that we forget to listen to those around us. We all see the world differently, and interpret things differently. This is why understanding an intention is important. Try to understand why they are doing what they are doing. We all deserve to be heard, including you.

Frustration is normal, but it is how we handle it that can either fuel or dilute it. Be calm and receptive. Listen. Sympathize. Explain. Be reasonable.

You feel jealous

Comparing yourself to others only subdues your ability to find yourself. It's hard to not look at someone and think they are prettier, skinnier, smarter, nicer, or happier. Jealousy can happen with a boyfriend, sister, brother, friend, or just someone at school who has something you wish you had.

You start to resent someone and talk poorly about them because you wish to be them or want something they have.

It is important to remember that the grass isn't always greener on the other side.

We all have difficult things we are going through or things we don't like about ourselves. When we try to be someone else or have the desire, we aren't able to see who we are because our self-individuality is fogged by our desires to be or be like someone who is not us.

It is also important to know that we can become jealous of others because they mirror our greatest insecurities. For instance, if you wish you were more outgoing and someone is very personable we tend to not like them because they mirror that trait we envy. Be aware of this and, rather than getting distant with someone for something they didn't mean to do, try to fix it within yourself. Either work on the characteristics this person mirrors within yourself or just be happy with those things that make *you* special.

You are here to just be *you*. You can't possibly be anyone else and nobody can be you. You must learn to be happy for the people you are jealous of. Train yourself to be excited for them- and yourself. Enjoy the person you are. Be who you are meant to be.

You feel like bad things keep happening to you

Sometimes we find ourselves stuck in a tornado as different things keep getting thrown into your funnel of life. A tornado swirls about, summoning everything into its rotation as it creates utter destruction. Sometimes we become overwhelmed and trapped in our own tornado, and you may find yourself destroying everything in your path. Maybe a breakup, bad grade, argument, rumor, or loss comes your way and the difficult events keep building up.

It is easy to let these events make you angry and resentful. Sometimes you withdraw from your friends, family, or daily hobbies. We let these difficult events determine our destiny. We let these difficult events be our crutches, the things we fall back on. We let these difficult events be the reason for our poor attitudes. We let these difficult events define us and ultimately bring us down.

As we grow up, we are told "life isn't always fair"- that statement is false. Life *is* fair. You are only dealt what you can handle. There will be instances where your life will be harder than someone else's. But there will also be those times when others are going through something more difficult than you. Being able to learn from what you are dealt is what makes life fair. Letting adversity empower you and make you better is what makes life fair. Knowing that everything happens for a reason and you will be okay as long as you don't lose yourself in the process is what makes life fair.

We are all given hardships. They are different because they are meant to shape us all differently. If we were all given the same difficulties we would all be the alike. You have to let these events build your character and make you stronger. You have every right to be upset, angry, sad, or frustrated, but never let these become your character. It will get better. Life will get easier as you learn to deal with your hardships and let them empower you.

So feel the pain, the anger, the frustration. But most importantly, cry the tears. We have so many tears welled up inside of us that have to be released to relinquish our feelings. Tears are not a sign of weakness, but a sign of strong feelings. So feel your emotions but don't forget to take the lesson from your hardship and add it to your jar of wisdom because your hardships no longer define you. It is not what happens to you, but how you react to what happens that makes you who you are and defines your character.

You I *will* get through it, and you are greater than your tornado.

Step out.

You feel like hopes and dreams are not for you

Sometimes you look around and see people that aspire to go to Ivy League colleges like Harvard, Yale, and Stanford. You see people who plan to study abroad. You see people who get a starting position on a sports team, becoming drum majors, or winning elections for different clubs. You see people around you pursuing amazing dreams but you feel like those things are out of reach for you.

This is a normal feeling, but you can do anything you want in life. No successful person got to where they are by luck. Each of them had hopes and dreams that drove them to their destiny. Everyone has them, but they are all different.

Maybe prestige colleges aren't for you, but maybe you want to travel the world! Maybe you want to go on mission trips. Everyone is entitled to their own dreams and aspirations whether it is a certain career, the arts, or sports. Find hopes and dreams that fit you and make you excited to try and accomplish them.

In life, people may tell you that you are dreaming too big or that you can't reach your goals. I will be the first to tell you to not listen to those people, no matter whom they are, *you* control your future. If you want something- do it. Dreams don't work unless you do, but there's nothing to work for if you don't have them.

Sometimes you may not form lofty goals because you are not encouraged to do so. This could be because loved ones are afraid to see you get hurt. It is hard to watch the ones you love not achieve their dreams, but failure is a reality. How you deal with it determines whether you are successful or not. Other times, people may be jealous, and therefore don't want to see you succeed. This is a hard concept to grasp, but it definitely happens. Never let anyone get in the way of your aspirations.

Someone has to do it. Why can't it be you?

Dream because dreaming is magical. Achieve because achieving feels good. Shoot for the moon because you are capable of everything you want to be capable of. Be the one to do it because someone has to.

You feel like people don't like you

Everyone has conflict. It doesn't matter who you are or how you were raised, we all have people throughout our lives that we butt heads with. People may say stuff behind your back, to your face, start rumors, or brutally harass you. But we can't focus on those few people hurting us. We must divert our attention to the plethora of people who love us.

We all have different personalities, and sometimes personalities clash. These clashes can be large or small, but either size has the power to make us feel like we are not liked.

This is normal.

Because we are all different, we respond to situations in various ways. This can tend to leave us feeling defeated. But don't be defeated. You are stronger than that.

What did you do wrong?

Think about your part in the conflicts you have with people. The best way to build character and fill your jar of wisdom is by learning from mistakes. Accept your part. But understand that it happens to all of us.

There are going to be people in your life that don't like you, it never makes harassment okay, but look at who loves you.

You are strong and you are loved. Don't be defeated. We all have our haters, but it is the effect we let them have on us that shows our character. Focusing on the negatives is what makes us feel heavy and disliked, so direct your mind to more positive thoughts and realize that there are always people who currently care or who are waiting to care about you.

You feel like you are not good at anything

At some point or another we all begin to feel down. You feel like you aren't good at anything. You see people who might be really good at sports, school, or music. Yet, we feel like there is nothing we are good at. You start to think you have no purpose because you have no talent.

You are absolutely wrong. The only problem is that you haven't found it yet.

We are all born with a particular purpose. With some of us, it just takes a little longer to find it. But part of finding your purpose and your passion is to know what your strengths are.

We all have strengths and weaknesses. But focus on your *strengths*. Write them somewhere where you will frequently see them. Never forget them.

Nobody is perfect and we can all better ourselves, but acknowledging those traits that make you unique is just as important.

Choose to see the strengths within yourself and always understand that you are special. People are waiting to see you succeed. One day you *will* come across your passion. In the meantime, acknowledge your strengths. You might be good at school, a sport, an instrument, giving advice, planning events, knowing things about life, religion. Everyone has different strengths.

You feel like you are not popular

What is popularity? Popularity is being well known and liked. In school, sometimes we tend to give popularity a new meaning. It becomes an adjective people strive to have attached to their name. Sometimes, in wanting to be popular, people do mean things to others. An example is when someone makes fun of one of their peers in front of a group of people. They do this so people will laugh at their joke- granted it is at someone else's expense. They do this to become liked and known.

Everyone wants to feel important and accepted. So the best way to feel important and accepted is to accept yourself. Being liked isn't a bad thing but it becomes bad when you are liked for the wrong reasons by the wrong people. So instead be liked by the right people for the right reasons.

School is a place to shape your future and who you are going to be. Instead of worrying about others liking you, focus on being comfortable with who you are. It is impossible to be constructive when you are being destructive. Popularity can blind you to what you're really doing. You stop noticing how you are treating others because you are so worried about being popular.

Find the people who accept you and make you feel good about yourself. Find the people who like you for being you and for being kind. Surround yourself with people who share interests with you and who encourage you. Being popular does not make you happy- but being yourself does. Be unique, and be the best you. Be known, liked, and respected for the right reasons and by the right people.

You feel like you are surrounded by drama

When you go through life, there are always places you go or situations you get into that seem to be full of pessimism and endless issues. Sometimes people say bad things about you- people you thought were your friends. Other times, people may be saying things about others. You seem to get caught in this endless path to nowhere.

You are the decision maker in your life. Choose to step out. As hard as it is, sometimes we must come to realize who our true friends are. People change, we change. Don't ever settle for friends who do not make you feel good.

Be you and surround yourself with the people that lift you up. Those people are out there. Sometimes they are hard to find, but the right friends are anxiously awaiting your company.

Other times in life, drama is inevitable. We all have different approaches to life and therefore sometimes don't agree with others. Also, we are all human and make mistakes or act out of character. In these cases it is best to make sure to not get involved. People will do things that frustrate you and make you want to do things you know are not right. Don't stray from your character and proper judgment. It is hard to not be reactionary but it can save you from unnecessary confrontation and burned bridges with people. For instance, if a friend does something you don't agree with or says something to offend you, don't speak poorly of them. Instead, talk to them about it. Communicate, don't hate.

Hate in your heart will consume you. Hatred leads to drama and drama really wears on people. So do what you know is right, even in times where you want to go against your better judgment.

Drama will never go away but it is all how you handle it. Instead of following with pessimism, lead with optimism.

You feel like you do not matter

I t is normal to feel like you do not matter. You may look around and you don't believe anyone cares about what you're going through. You sometimes feel nobody knows your story and why you are the way you are. Everyone seems to have a perfect life and you're nothing but another person in a confused society of peers trying to find their way.

Sometimes things get bad. We feel pain and want to give up because it feels like life is too hard and nobody even cares. But I promise you that it gets better. If you can get past your lowest lows, you will see your purpose.

Your lows teach you lessons so you don't have to encounter that same low ever again. As you learn more lessons you are able to overcome more, allowing you to see more clear. When we see clear we see our purpose and why you *do* matter. So don't let these lows get to you because you have so much more awaiting.

We are all going down our own paths that consist of pain and tears, but you *do* matter. It doesn't matter who you are, you are leaving a mark on someone's life- you may not even know it.

You were put on this planet to be you. Nobody else can do what you have the potential to do. Nobody can have the particular passion you are inclined to behold. You matter more than you know. Be grateful you're here. Be excited to explore your passions. Be inspired to pursue your future.

Use your jar of wisdom to find your happiness.

You feel like your friends do not care about you

We go through ups and downs in life. No matter the level of perfection some seem, we all fall. In life, we are supposed to surround ourselves with those who will catch us when we fall, who will support us when times are bad. But sometimes we get lost. We begin befriending people who make us feel cool and popular for the wrong reasons, people who want to bring us down, people who eat at our insecurities, people who walk away when we fall. These are the people that do not care about you.

Find those who care and who will catch you.

In school, we are all searching for our souls, at times making us selfish. There are two kinds of selfishness in school: selfishness to promote our own popularity or selfishness to focus on who we are and discover our unique paths in life. Some choose to fit in, and a few choose to take their own path. Dare to be different and choose to be selfish in taking care of you. Surround yourself with those who love you and truly care, not those who are on an endless pursuit to find popularity.

Find yourself and what you stand for and surround

yourself with those who support that, and who extend their arms when you fall. There are always people who care but, because we are all different, we all need different things in a friend. Your idea of a friend may be different from mine. So find the friends that make you feel good and fit your definition.

And remember- when people bring you pain, vow to not do to others what they have done to you, add it to you jar of wisdom and surround yourself with people who bring you bliss.

You feel like your peers have better lives

It is normal to look at someone and feel like things are better for them. But we all have our stories. All of us suffer from one thing or another.

One of the interesting aspects of life is the fact that we all see it through different eyes. We all see from unique perspectives. This makes for people having varied reactions to different events in life. Some of us mask our pain and others of us wear our emotions vibrantly. So it may look as though someone has a better life but it doesn't mean they do. Life is what you make of it. It isn't about what you are dealt but it is about what you make of what you have. The grass is not always greener on the other side, so make the most of the side you're standing on.

It is through green eyes of envy that we see our greatest insecurities. If you aren't happy, take a step back, revise your life and make change.

Life is all about reactions. A million bad things can happen and knock you down but do you get back up? Bad things happen to all of us but what shows character is how we react. If someone says something rude to you, do you say something rude back or remain kind and compassionate?

Bad things *will* happen but what differentiates happy from sad and weak from strong, is our reactions to these situations. Let your struggles empower you. You are much greater than the things you have to go through. Make the most of everything you have. Instead of waiting for the good times to come to you, create them.

You feel lonely

I t is easy to become lonely when you aren't like everyone else. In school, people tend to conform to those around them to fit in. Those of us that decide we don't want to conform are stuck feeling alone and left out. Sometimes you ponder what it would be like to be like everyone else and fit in. Or maybe you are currently trying to fit in and are coming to realize you want to be unique but are afraid of being lonely.

Remember that being unique is a beautiful thing. At times it is good to be alone and learn more about yourself.

Having alone time is the perfect opportunity to pursue your passions. Spend your time doing the things you love to do: drawing, playing sports, or even playing board games. Some other ways to allot this time is to spend it serving others, get a job, or join a club. Find a way to get involved in your community or to meet other like-minded individuals. Being lonely is not being by yourself. Being lonely is having the opportunity to express who you are. You get time to find things you enjoy doing, and to find other friendships in people that are like you.

In some cases, you may be ousted by a group of

people, in which case you would begin to feel lonely. People don't want to be around others that aren't doing the same thing because sometimes they may be embarrassed about their actions or fear you will judge them. Don't try to defend your cause. Instead, invest your time in activities you love to do and people who really care to understand you.

Sometimes we focus too much on being "in" that we forget to be us. Find where you can be both: accepted and being yourself.

You feel unhappy with your appearance

I t is so easy to look in a mirror and find a million things wrong with the image that appears. We are our own worst enemy. We see things that remain unapparent to a peer's eye. We deteriorate our self-confidence.

There are always things to do to improve the way you look. Eating healthy and exercising are two things you commonly hear that aid in gaining self-confidence. This is true. Find an eating plan that is maintainable and gives you all the necessary nutrition to stay healthy and energized. Exercise is all about personal preference. It is important to be active, but find your own unique way to do it. I love martial arts, yoga, and running. What makes you feel good?

Aside from eating healthy and exercising, being confident with who you are and what you look like is most definitely a mind game.

Another reason you may be unhappy with your appearance is because you are comparing your own to someone else's. Comparison is the thief of joy. When we compare we see everything we want in ourselves, but become blind to our beauties. Instead of looking at what you don't have, look at what you do because that person you are comparing yourself to is most likely comparing themselves to someone as well.

We are all born beautiful in many, many ways. Try writing down your strengths and putting them somewhere where you frequently look such as: a mirror, wall, or agenda. Being confident begins within.

Personality shines brighter than white teeth. Remind yourself why you are special. Rather than being your biggest critic be your biggest advocate.

How To

How to be a leader

Through the course of our lives, we frequently encounter things that make us uncomfortable. These things could be heights, talking in front of large groups, traveling, socializing with people you don't know, asking questions in class, etc.

The best way to become a leader and grow as a person is to experience these things that put us outside of our comfort zones. Do the things that frighten you.

This is not as much about conquering your fears as it is about broadening your life spectrum. The more we do and face, the more things we are able to do in life. Think back to your first day of school. The first time you went you were terrified. By taking that scary step though, you are able to come to school every day feeling good.

Leaders have to take these scary steps first. I challenge you to step outside of your comfort zone because once you do, others will follow.

Never forget that the goal of leading is to create more leaders and to inspire others to be confident enough in who they are to reach their full potential. Leading to gain followers creates falsified fronts. When you lead to gain followers, it shows that you are being selfish in your pursuits. Meaning you don't have other's best interest in mind. Leading to inspire other leaders means that you are modeling sincerity. You are setting an example and inspiring those around you by treating them as equals.

Leading is not a position, but a lifestyle. Leading is not being fake so the most people will like you, it is being sincere and comfortable with whom you are to inspire people to want to do the same.

How to be strong

We all go through a lot in life, and sometimes things get really hard. It's easy to have negative thoughts and think that this is the end. People may tell you, "be strong" but what does that mean? Do I have to conceal all my emotions? Do I act like this doesn't bother me? Do I let people hurt me?

Being strong is not letting adversity define you. We are human. We need to feel pain. When we feel strongly it is vital to cry sometimes. Tears are not a sign of weakness but they show that you feel passionately about something.

How do you not let your struggles define you?

Learning lessons from the troubles we face and adding them to our jars of wisdom defines us. It is so important to not use a struggle as a crutch. Don't let them be your excuse for failure. Let adversity be your reason for success.

Think about the things you go through, what can you do to avoid them next time? Maybe you need to befriend different people or make more wise decisions. But sometimes there is no lesson to be taken, like with a death. It is hard to draw lessons from it but you can let it empower you. Allow all of the pains you endure build your character and give you a reason to want to enjoy life.

Being strong is not masking your feelings. Being strong is feeling pain and crying if you need, but letting it all make you a better person in the long run.

Remember that your life isn't over. You have downs and hit rock bottom, but from there you can only go up. Time heals all wounds.

You must experience your worst times in order to feel your best times. Feeling those worst times then overcoming them and taking the lesson to reach the good times is what strength is all about.

How to be unique

Many people tell you, "be unique" or "don't be like the rest of the crowd". But how do you do this?

To be unique, let all of your colors shine through. Be exactly who you are- every strange, enthralling aspect of you. To do this you must be confident. You have to have your own mindset, style, hobbies, and favorites. Being unique means that, rather than going along with everyone else, you are confident enough to live life your own way. Start by trying new things. You'll never know what you like until you try it. Be adventurous and sporadic! Do what makes you happy. Being unique also means being okay with standing up for who you are. You have to let the haters hate and do what you know is right.

There is a quote, "be a fruit loop in a bowl of cheerios". This is very true, yet it leaves out an important part. It is so important to be you. You are not going to be like everyone else, because everyone is brought up different. So do not try to shrink yourself to fit in. Instead, be you. Be comfortable being you.

Standing out is good because it allows you to be who

you are. Nothing can beat the happiness and content being unique brings you. Yet, don't let uniqueness isolate you. Be a fruit loop in a bowl of cheerios, but don't let it make you lonely. Surround yourself with other fruit loops that will make you feel accepted and help you to aspire to be an even better version of yourself.

Being unique is not easy, especially in the beginning. But it pays off because you get to live your life exactly the way you want to live it.

How to deal with harassment

I t hurts more than anything when people mistreat us. We start to think: *is it my fault? What have I done? How can I stop this?*

Maybe people are spreading false rumors- you feel like everyone is talking about you and nobody has your back. You feel hopeless and crushed. Maybe people are saying things to you over the internet or to your face. You feel like you can't tell someone about it or confront the bully. Instead, you take the blows, as you just deteriorate inside.

Stop right there. You are way stronger than you think.

Maybe you have done something. Learn from your mistake. But nobody deserves to be hurt. That is not your fault. Harassment is not okay. People are mean because they don't feel good about themselves. They bring others down to build themselves up. Do not let anyone drag you down. You are amazing. You are unique. Learn from your mistakes. Grow. Stay strong. If you need to tell an adult, do so. Yet, sometimes that can make things worse. The ball is in your court. Next time somebody treats you poorly, take the high road. When people are doing you wrong, it is because something is not right within them. Reach out to them. This act will surprise them and make them take a step back. Be kind. You are not a victim. Most importantly, never be mean back. Two wrongs never make a right.

Let pain make you stronger. For you are stronger than you think. People cannot drag you in any direction without your permission. Rise above, learn from your mistakes, grow from theirs, and add the lessons to your jar of wisdom.

How to enjoy the life you have

Life gets hard. We all experience ups and downs. It is often that we find ourselves lingering in the downs while life is giving us so many opportunities to go up. It is easy to not see what all we have to enjoy around us, but more fulfilling to enjoy our lives.

The best way to remain positive and appreciative of life is to not rely on others to make you happy. You are the only one who can make you happy. It isn't up to anything or anyone but you to do so. There are so many beautiful things along your pursuit of happiness; you just have to look harder sometimes.

With every dark moment comes a sliver of light. That sliver of light appears much smaller than the darkness that can envelop us, but focus on that light and move towards it. It becomes greater and helps you ignore the negativity. For instance, you may be getting bullied by a peer but rather than focusing on the negativity, you can realize that there are more people around you that love you than those who don't. Focus on the people who support you and want to see you succeed rather than that person or few people who are trying to trap you in darkness.

To enjoy your life as a whole, it's important to enjoy the little pieces. When we live in the moment, it helps us to not depend on the future to bring happiness. In order to love the life you are living, love the people, the memories, the magic engulfing you, and the mini moments of laughter you share with those who bring bliss to your life. You must love little to love big.

To be happy with now, you must be yourself. It doesn't matter what other people think! Explore the world and be yourself. Be too concerned on improving and loving your life to worry about negativity.

Look at the positives in each situation, whether it looks like taking the lessons out of mistakes or dancing in rainstorms, enjoy the little moments, and just being who you are!

How to find and pursue your passions

Everyone is brought up differently. The environments in which we grow up differ from that of anyone else. The way we are taught to handle situations in life are all different. All of us are also born with traits and characteristics that define us by the way we react and interact. On top of that, we all learn diverse lessons that make our jars of wisdom all unique. Because of these factors, we all have our own unique passions. Sometimes it is hard to identify them if you do not know how to look.

Passions are what make us successful because they bring bliss. A passion is something that you love to do, something that fulfills you.

In life, you will come across something that makes you want to work harder, something that inspires you to persevere and accomplish everything set in front of you. These are your passions. Act on them.

Passions are different for everyone such as helping others, playing a sport, designing clothes, drawing, or innovating. There are so many possibilities!

When you find yours, you will want to do nothing

but pursue it. Your path to doing so is unique to your passion. Plant the seed by setting your goals and begin to grow your happiness. Tend to those young seedlings: water them, and nourish them by continuing to indulge in your beloved activities. Grow as many as you can! Passions are vital because they give us new meaning. They give us our individualism.

Find them.

Pursue them.

Live a prosperous life full of passion.

How to get good grades

I t is so hard to not get down on yourself when your grades are not where they are supposed to be. You feel stupid or dumb. You get a test back and you flip your paper over so nobody has to see your grade. As everyone talks about their 'A' or 'B', you sink down in your chair as your cheeks feel hot and turn rosy red.

To get good grades, you do not have to be the most intelligent person at your school. This might sound absurd, but I promise. To get good grades, you need to have dedication and you must work hard. Colleges are looking for people that do not give up, for people that have excellent work ethics, and for all around genuine people.

Work to your potential. If you are working to your full potential, amazing things will happen. Do the best you can do. That is all anyone expects: teachers, parents, colleges, peers, etc.

Working to your full potential in school is extremely important. It may seem pointless and you may get aggravated, but it is rewarding in the long run. When you do all that you can, you get a sense of accomplishment in return, a fulfillment only you can induce. Working hard in school teaches you to work hard in other areas as well. The more you practice this, the easier and more natural it will become.

Sometimes we can work to our full potential but still won't be getting straight A's. That is okay. We don't all excel in school. Everyone has their talents and areas where they excel.

If you do your best, you will get good grades. This may not mean a 4.0, but they will be the best you can do- and that is all anyone ever wants.

How to handle making a mistake

Sometimes in life, we make mistakes. Everyone makes them- big or small. You aren't alone. When you know you have made a mistake, you feel disappointed in yourself. Sometimes you think people are going to dislike you for your mistakes- and they may. It feels like you've reached a dead end and will forever be defined by your mistakes.

Well, let me tell you, your mistakes are nothing but learning experiences. The first step to growing from your mistakes, is acknowledging you have made one. If you are reading this, you have acknowledged it. We all mess up. Being able to apologize to yourself, or someone you have affected, will immediately relinquish the strike of your mistake.

Apologies take guts, and a good person. Once you have apologized and acknowledged what you have done, reflect and take the lesson from your mistake. Realize what you did and don't do it again. We make mistakes to grow as individuals. Everyone makes different mistakes because we are meant to be shaped in our own unique ways.

Yet sometimes we make big mistakes. Big mistakes

that alter the course our life is on. Maybe you have committed a crime, been caught drinking or smoking, or maybe you were suspended. It is hard to forgive yourself after something like this because we frequently begin to think we aren't better than our weakest moments. This is false, completely false. If you want to be a better person all of the power resides in you. You *can* do it. I believe in you and so do other people that you may not even realize.

These big mistakes must start with a commitment to you. Vow to yourself that you will do whatever it takes to be that person you truly want to be. This may entitle getting help, maybe from a counselor, a teacher, or a parent; whoever it may be, let them help you. I can promise you they have made a mistake as well.

You can come back. It will be hard. It will take time. And you will want to quit. But don't let your negative self-talk get the best of you. You are strong and you are special, so don't let these moments define you. Let them alter your life, not because you got in trouble, but because you were given an opportunity to grow and be the you, you want to be.

Your mistakes don't define you, but they help build you and reward you with lessons to add to your jar of wisdom. Mistakes are meant to be made. Mistakes are not the seed of your character but rather the riches that water it. You only attain these riches by pulling out the lessons. And always remember- you are only human.

How to handle social media

I have had Twitter, Facebook, Instagram, and Tumblr. I have seen and experienced enough on social media to know that it takes a large toll on teenagers. Yes, it can be good to reconnect with people and for advertisement and such, but how many teenagers actually do that?

We become so enthralled with what everyone else is doing, that we don't focus on ourselves. We find it so much more interesting to compare picture favorites to following ratios than to enjoy life. We forget what it is like to talk with someone in person; instead we just tweet at them.

Social media is a mask for bullies. It is an easy place to harass people without anyone knowing who it is. Or sometimes people become more comfortable saying rude things when they aren't looking you in the eye.

Social media lessens our ability to live in the riches of right now. Instead we live in the past and wonder what could have been instead of putting your phone down and realizing what is right in front of you. When you are engulfed in social media you cannot love the life you have.

I ask that you think about social media. What are you gaining from it? If you know how to stay positive and not let an app consume you, that is amazing! But if you aren't able to do that- disconnect. It is okay to not be constantly accessible. Do what is ultimately going to positively benefit you the most.

How to know if you are successful

Many of us get lost in a misconstrued definition of success. I know I did. It is important to understand that success is not materialistic, but rather intangible. Success is measured by happiness.

Success is frequently thought of as someone who has a lot of money. This may bring some people happiness, but it isn't the general scheme. Success is when you feel content and proud of where you are in life. In order to be successful you must enjoy the little moments as you shoot for your dreams. Find fun in all you do. Achieving your goals can be tough but don't let it consume you, you must relish in the journey in order to be happy.

That being said, everyone has different goals. Maybe you want to be a teacher, coach, doctor, marine biologist, chef, or make your own business. Maybe you want to make the top team in a sport, learn to play your favorite instrument, or run a marathon. Success is the act in which we accomplish goals that bring us happiness.

We know we are successful when we feel proud of ourselves and content in our surroundings. You might feel successful from finding the right friends, and another might enjoy the success of building a billion dollar company.

You know you are successful when you can wake up in the morning with a smile, content about what you have done, what you have learned from trial and error, content about today and content with where you have directed yourself with the help of your goals.

How to make sure you are enjoying your life

We all get busy. We overload ourselves to get into college, help others, achieve our goals, make sure we are getting good grades, and much, much more. Yet, we tend to get so caught up in the flow of life that we forget to remember what makes *us* happy.

To make sure you are enjoying your life, think about everything you are doing. Make a list. Go through and make sure that everything you are doing is fulfilling you in some way. If it isn't, cross it out. You must take care of you. Don't do things that you don't like. And don't be afraid to stop doing something that doesn't make you happy

It can be hard because you don't want to upset people, but there comes a time when you have to learn to do what is best for *you*. For example, if you are doing a sport that you realize you don't enjoy anymore- don't do it. Yes it is hard because your parents most likely have been paying for it, but they want your happiness more than anything and that is what is most important.

In order to get to a point where you can help others and enjoy the world around you, you have to make sure you are doing things that lift you up. Life is too short to live just to please others.

Success is being happy and content. Take out the things you don't enjoy and create your own success. Happiness is not circumstantial- it is finding happiness in every circumstance.

How to manage your time

Managing your time correctly can be the hardest part of being a teenager. We are pulled in so many different directions and sometimes it is hard to make everyone happy while taking care of you.

To begin, write down everything you have to do, even the little things. It is very satisfying to accomplish something. Every time you complete a task on your list check it off, and take a second to exhale and relax.

Break up your work and don't do it all at once to make sure you aren't harboring unnecessary stress. Estimate the time it will take to do every task so you can make an accurate schedule.

Staying healthy is a vital part of managing your time. If you are too tired, you won't be able to stay awake. If you are hungry, you won't be able to concentrate. If you don't feel good about yourself, you will be more lackadaisical. Take care of you so you can be the best you.

Last, make sure to include time to have fun. Do something that takes your mind off of the stresses you have. It is important to enjoy the life you live.

In managing your time, there are going to be tasks, like washing the dishes, which you don't want to do. But try telling yourself you want to. Your mindset is yours; therefore you are the only one with the power to change it and your mind is very powerful.

Organize, take care of your body, and reward yourself.

How to not let high school change you for the worse

Going into high school is a big step in life. High school has the power to change you for the better or for the worse. It is the gateway to your freedom. The choices you make will point you in the direction for the future.

Be you. Make your own decisions, but never judge someone else's.

When you conform to those around you that is when you are letting it change you for the worse. People will try to peer pressure you into things- make your own decisions. Nobody knows you better than yourself. There will be times when you think to against your better judgment or maybe you act upon those thoughts. But learn from those times so you don't become defined by your mistakes, pulling you far away from all your potential.

In order to let high school change you for the *best*, you must add to and use your jar of wisdom. Let the hard times make you stronger: the mistakes, the harassment, the jealousy, and the negative self-talk. You will only change for the better if you can learn from your worst times. And when you learn those lessons, you have to use them. If you learn that it wasn't right of you to treat someone the way you did, make sure to not do it again.

Some other ways to not let high school change you for the worse are to think positive and set goals. When you think negative, you become trapped by your weakest thoughts. So, instead of holding yourself back with negative self-talk, think positive. This is an important thing to do because when we talk negative to ourselves we become victims of self-imposed harassment, making us susceptible to peer pressure and acting out of character - the poisons of high school. Setting goals also keeps you on the right track because we are constantly aiming for something, not looking for trouble.

Always keep your goals in mind. Have fun and indulge in the life you have been given, because it is truly a gift. But don't let high school make you someone you are not or someone you will regret being.

Make a difference in your world wherever you go, inspire those around you. Be the best you, and don't let high school rob you of your identity. Instead, let it make you even better than you already are.

How to pick a career field in high school

Many people are constantly worried about what school they want to go to or what they want to do with their life. This is totally normal. There is so much pressure at school to make a decision on what you want to spend your life doing.

Stop. You do not have to know, I promise!

Our school years are meant to let us dip our toes into every kind of career field; whether we are into music, sports, science, math, literature, business etc.

It is important to know that your career will find you. Trying to force it may land you in a place you do not want to be. One day it will hit you, and I promise you that. Continue to experiment in various subjects until you find what you love and what makes you feel complete.

Sometimes it is a life experience, sudden opportunity, influential talk, or just someone who sees something special in you that will lead you to your passion. Until that point, just live and be unique. The events that happen on your journey to discovering your future will fall into your jar of wisdom. Eventually that jar will lead you down a lively path to your future.

The best thing about education is that you do not have to know exactly where you are headed; you just have to have a direction.

How to read someone's story

We all have a story. By that I mean we are all the way we are because of the things that have either happened or not happened to us. Each person's story is different. They show us how to interact with one another in a positive manner.

Healthy interaction with others stems from knowing one's intentions. Intentions can be good or bad, but they have the power to alter communication between two people. Knowing your own intentions is important so you can properly address a situation. When you know your intentions are positive, you can take notice of someone else's.

Why is someone acting the way they are? We can answer this question by reading their story.
You must take precautions because these stories can be powerful, personal, or peaceful.

Some don't want to take time to get to know people and that is okay. It is a personal preference. I like to know who I am surrounding myself with, whether they are an acquaintance or best friend.

We all begin reading a book by examining the cover.

Look at how people act: the way they carry themselves, the way they look at and treat others, how they handle life's highs and lows.

Next, we take a glance at the author: who wrote the book? Notice someone's family, who their friends are, what classes they take, what sports they play. Paying attention to who and what someone surrounds them self with and looking at the factors that have made them who they are, are important keys to understanding them.

We then read the back. Take the time to approach someone. Make casual conversation, let their charisma envelop you.

After that, we begin reading. Dive deeper in conversations. Listen to their opinions. Sympathize with their adversity. Be interested and let people know you care and they will want to open up.

As people open up to us, we begin to unravel their story, piece together their puzzle.

Then, and only then, will you be able to understand why they are the way they are. We can better determine their intentions, to help us in communication.

Even bullies have a story. I strongly believe people are not born bad, some people just aren't taught how to handle various instances in their lives. It is never too late to turn things around. Life is full of chances and opportunities.

Read someone's story- they are all interesting.

How to relieve your stress

Relieving stress is vital no matter what age you are. We get caught up in the anxiety of life, thoughts constantly crowding our minds. Take a breather. Give yourself an outlet where you can forget everything.

The best way to find something to relieve your stresses is to find something you love to do. Not only that, but find a hobby that allows you to block everything else out of your train of thought, where you can express yourself and your feelings without having to think about it. This sounds absurd, but each and every one of us has one of these outlets. Maybe it is drawing, painting, running, a sport, hiking, meditating, yoga, etc.

Give yourself time every day to do that task, whatever it may be.

This also gives you time to investigate yourself. What do you find soothing? What does that say about you? How does this reflect your passions? Being able to answer these questions is important, as you slowly begin to develop yourself.

Another way to relieve your stress is by blocking out

negative self- talk. So many times we get caught up in punishing ourselves or dwelling on mistakes and weaknesses. When you hear yourself thinking negatively, push that thought out of your head. Our most aggressive stressors are those negative views we have of ourselves. Instead of telling yourself you can't do something, tell yourself you can. Instead of telling yourself how stupid you just looked in front of those people, disregard it because those that matter don't mind and those that mind don't matter. Instead of stressing out about the little things, focus on constructive self- talks that truly matter. Tell yourself you *can* do it, no matter what *it* may be. You *can* attain your goals; you *can* be the person you want to be. Be confident in who you are and tell yourself you enjoy life's amenities.

Stress is avoidable. Give yourself breaks whether mental, physical, or both.

How to see your big picture

Your big picture becomes apparent by taking a step back and looking at the world as a panorama. Look at all of society's triumphs and failures. See the way the world works and how everyone fits in. Seeing your big picture means seeing where you fit into that panorama. What are you going to do to better yourself and others? Where do you belong? What are you meant to do?

The most important part about seeing the big picture is realizing that everyone's is different.

Now that you know how to begin seeing your big picture, you must learn how to develop it.

What are your passions?

Your passions are reflections on who you are and what brings you ultimate bliss. Take your passions and find how you can share them with your friends, family, community, and then the world. Your passions are what you love- they are extensions of your soul. Make the world love them and care about them as much as you, no matter what they are. You are the only one with this power.

We hold so much power as individuals. We can do

anything from changing a light bulb to changing the world. Use your jar of wisdom and your passions to guide you through the world's panorama to find where you fit.

How to set goals

Setting small goals is important to keep you on track for your larger goals. The little goals keep us accountable to make sure we are maintaining sight of our lofty goals.

The smaller goals may consist of things such as doing your homework every day for a week, then two weeks, then a month. These goals help you achieve your overall, larger goals.

The overarching goal that encompasses the more minute ones must be construed from your passions and your big picture. After you know where you fit in the world and what your passions are, you can set large goals that you want to achieve.

With each large goal, you are finding various ways to express your passions and concoct creative ideas to cater to where you view yourself in our world's panorama. Take into account that the larger the goal you set, the more you push yourself. And the best part about it is that everyone's goals will be completely different. Let your big goals be reflections of you. Let them pull you forward in your pursuit of happiness and expression.

Shoot for the sun and be exceptionally proud getting to explore different planets. Take your goals to the next level. They are yours because only *you* can achieve them. Your purpose is not my purpose, and mine is not yours. We are all different people with different reasons for living. Set your large goals. You will experience failure, but the best of us do. Learn from your failures, fill your jar of wisdom, and be content with where you land.

Goals are your North Star. Let them lead you but be proud of wherever you decide to branch off. It's okay to wander, that's how we discover Earth's greatest amenities.

Don't grant anyone the opportunity to hold you back, because you are capable. You can do anything you dream to achieve. Life is your canvas- paint it in ways that allow you to be happy and express yourself. Begin by setting your big goals and then set smaller goals that will build up to that large goal.

Note to Readers

Remember that you are special. You are loved. You are unique. And you are meant to be on this planet to serve a purpose, a purpose nobody else on this planet can serve because you are you, and nobody is better at being you than you yourself. You can't be anyone else. Take your passions and create your own destiny.

Your goals are waiting for you to exceed them. Life is hard at times. It is cruel and dark but it is also is magical. Our world is special and fair in its own, unique way. The world is amazing but it is easy to become consumed in a tornado. But know when to jump out and let the swirl of anger, selfishness, hate, and bitterness keep going. Once you step out of your tornado, it no longer is what people see when they look at you. It stays with you but is not *you*.

When you use your hardships as crutches it calls forth your tornado. Walk away from your tornado and create your own path. It will be scary. It will be hard. But it will also be magical, rewarding, and ultimately it will be full of joy and happiness because you know that you turned your back on adversity and let yourself become who you are meant to be who you are. So feel the pain, the hurt, and the grief and keep walking towards your goals. NEVER STOP.

It's okay to ask for help along the way. You can't do it all on your own. Mistakes and hardships are meant to happen but what you do with them is what makes you who you're going to be. If you let them join your tornado, you won't become who you're meant to be. If you pull the lessons and put them in your jar of wisdom, you will have the ingredients for your success.

I challenge you to live a life of your own success and build a beautiful life around you in this magical world.

What is magical about our world?

Love
Passion
Being able to see through eyeballs
Being able to touch your surroundings
Running water
Lightening
Blooming flowers
Having a nose that enables you to smell beautiful scents
Having small little feet that support your weight every day
Being able to grow hair
Not knowing where exactly the universe is
The fact that life itself makes no sense
Tasting food
Being able to talk and communicate
Sea creatures that can breathe underwater
Thumbs
Color
We are all born with talents
The human brain
Books that let you experience another world
Diversity
The ability to feel emotions
Electricity
Being able to have any question answered on Google
The Grand Canyon
Being able to capture a moment of time with pictures

What would you say is magical about our world? I recommend making your own list to keep with you, and let it be a constant reminder of the positivity that envelops you.

15559894R00050

Made in the USA
San Bernardino, CA
30 September 2014